My Family and Me

# Welcoming a New Baby

## Mary Auld

SEA-TO-SEA

*Mankato  Collingwood  London*

It is a very special time when a new baby is born. It is the start of a new life.

**?** Your turn...

What was the date of your birth? How long have you been alive?

A baby grows inside its mom's tummy for nine months before it is born. The whole family gets ready for the baby's arrival.

" Zoe says...

"I used to talk to my baby brother inside my mom's tummy—although I didn't know he was a boy then!"

Most babies are born in a
hospital. Families often go
to visit them there.

Billy and Olive took presents for their mom and the new baby.

Your turn...

What present would you give a new baby?

Some babies are born early and are too small to go home for a while. Their mom helps look after them in the hospital.

Marco says...
"I was born early. My mom spent all the time she could with me until I was strong enough to go home."

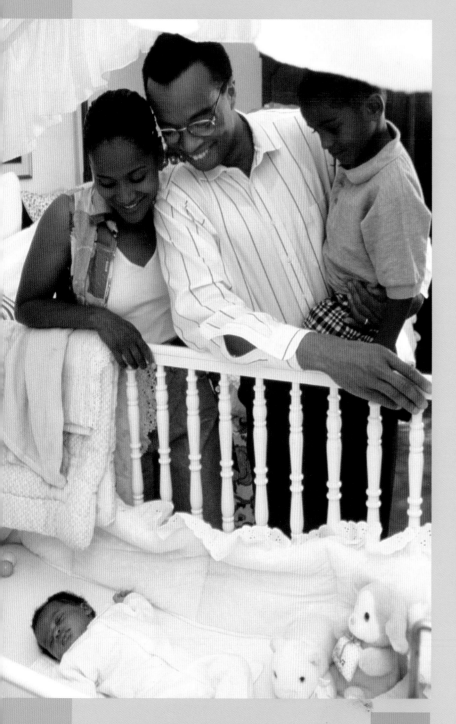

It's exciting bringing a new baby home.

Ed and his family made his new sister's room just right.

Maria's grandma came to stay for a few days to help out.

Your turn...

Who helped look after you when you were a baby?

Everyone in the family is busy
with a new baby around.

Raj and
Anita help
feed their
brother.

# Leo helps his dad change his baby sister's diaper.

66 Leo says...
"I try to make Rosie laugh while
Dad puts her clothes back on."

Everyone likes to kiss and cuddle a baby to say hello.

When Paul's parents first adopted him, they held him all the time.

14

Emma likes to cuddle up on the sofa with her family.

**Your turn...**
Have you ever held a baby?
What did it feel like?

Many people have special
ceremonies to name a baby.
Sky's parents planted a tree at
her naming ceremony.

Daniel was named at his baptism. Everyone welcomed him into the Christian religion.

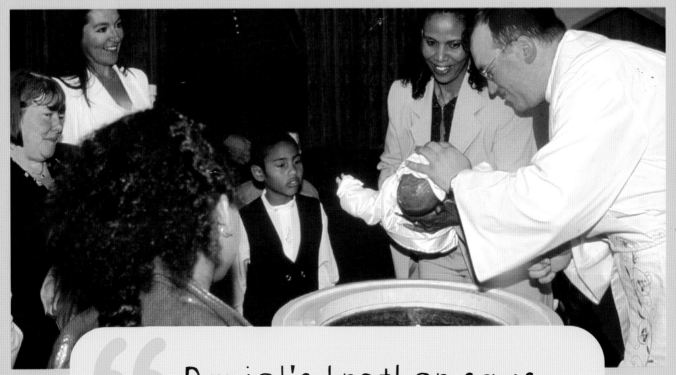

"

Daniel's brother says...
"He was good and didn't cry, even when the priest put water on his head."

There are many other special ceremonies to welcome a new baby. Rajinder's family bounced him in candies during the Sikh festival of Lohi.

? Your turn...
Did your family have a special ceremony to welcome you?

Babies grow up quickly. We celebrate the day we were born every year—on our birthday.

> **Neil says...**
>
> "On my birthday, Grandpa always says he remembers me when **I** was no bigger than a flea!"

How would you
welcome a new baby
to your family?

# Some Things to Do

Ask your parents what you were like when you were a baby. What do they remember about the first time you came home?

With your friends, make a collection of pictures of all of you as babies. Can you recognize who is who?

Make a list of all the different things you can think of that you need to do to look after a baby.

Write a poem or tell a story about the birth of a new baby.

## About this book

The aim of this book is to give children the opportunity to explore what their family means to them and their role within it in a positive and celebratory way. In particular it emphasizes the importance of care and support within the family. It also encourages children to compare their own experiences with other people, recognizing similarities and differences and respecting these as part of daily life.

Children will get pleasure out of looking at this book on their own. However, sharing the book on a one-to-one basis or within a group will also be very rewarding. Just talking about the main text and pictures is a good starting point, and the panels also prompt discussion:
• Question panels ask children to talk directly about their own experiences and feelings.
• Quote panels encourage them to think further by comparing their experiences with those of other children.

This edition first published in 2011 by
Sea-to-Sea Publications
Distributed by Black Rabbit Books
P.O. Box 3263, Mankato, Minnesota 56002

Printed in China, Dongguan

Library of Congress Cataloging-in-Publication Data

Auld, Mary.
  Welcoming a new baby / Mary Auld.
    p. cm. -- (My family and me)
  ISBN 978-1-59771-232-3 (library binding)
 1.  Infants--Family relationships--Juvenile literature. 2. Families--Juvenile literature.  I. Title.
  HQ774.A85 2011
  306.875083'2--dc22
                                        2009051544

9  8  7  6  5  4  3  2

Published by arrangement with the Watts Publishing Group Ltd, London.


Series editor: Rachel Cooke
Art director: Jonathan Hair
Design: Jason Anscomb

Picture credits: Paul Baldesare/Photofusion: 20. John Birdsall/John Birdsall Photo Library: 5, 8, 14, 15. Tim Dub/Photofusion: Cover, 2. Laura Dwight/Corbis: 11. ER Productions/Corbis: 6. Sally Greenhill/Sally & Richard Greenhill: 7, 12, 17. Judy Harrison/Photofusion: 13, 19. Hannah Marsh/John Birdsall Photo Library: 24. Chuck Savage/Corbis: 10. Mo Wilson/Photofusion:16. Every attempt has been made to clear copyright. Should there be any inadvertent omission please apply to the publisher for rectification.

Please note that some of the pictures in this book have been posed by models.

March 2010
RD/6000006414/002